TRACTS OF MY YEARS
AN ADDICTION TESTIMONY

TrubuPRESS is a subsidiary of the Trubu Media Group whose interests include but are not limited to fiction and non fiction stories from the black experience throughout the American and African Diaspora.

Publisher: TrubuPRESS
Editor: Neo Blaqness
Cover Design: TrubuPRESS
Cover Photo: Champaign News Gazette
Proofreader: Tamika Coleman

Tracts of My Years: An Addiction Testimony
Copyright © 2013 Frank J. Bradford

To order: Tracts of My Years: An Addiction Testimony
visit http://trubupress.com
or call (872) 22TRUBU

Booksellers:
Retail discounts are available from TrubuPRESS. Inquiries about volume orders can be made via the phone number listed above.

ISBN-13: 978-0615894898
ISBN-10: 0615894895
Published by TrubuPRESS

PRINTED IN THE UNITED STATES

DEDICATION

This book is dedicated to a multitude of people that are significant in my life. First, I give the honor to the Lord, who is the head of my life. This book is dedicated to my two Bishops, one in Champaign, IL and the other in Milwaukee, WI: Bishop Lloyd E. Gwin and Bishop Darrell L. Hines, respectively.

I believe that God has given them the wisdom to lead and the ability to recite what saith the Lord. To Evangelist Gwin, Pastor Pamela Hines, Pastor Theron Rogers Sr. , and Pastor Banks, who I feel that the Lord has blessed them to go out and win souls through their teaching.

This book is also dedicated to my wife, P. Utley Bradford, who is the queen of life and has been by my side for many years. My wife did not even know that I was an Ex-Addict until it leaked out and even then she stood by me before I turned to the Lord.

The dedication of this book also goes to my siblings, my older brother, Percy for putting his foot down and forcing me to leave cocaine alone with red in his eyes, my sister, Lillie, who listened first hand to my drug addict testimonies, and to my other brother,

C.R., who understood my dilemma and did not turn his back to me.

I also must dedicate this book to my last living uncles, L.T. who taught me how to drive a stick shift for the first time in a U.S. Postal van and for also being the manager of my R&B band.

I'd like to thank the person at that time, for putting a flute in my hands and taking time to teach me music and the fundamentals of the flute and Archie and Aunt Mary; all had significant gifts to pass along to me through my lifetime. The dedication of this book also goes to all of my children and grandchildren by birth and through marriage.

My last dedications of this book go to my sister-in-law, Cynthia Utley, my late mother-in law, Claudia Utley and to my mother and father and Uncle Charlie for giving me an opportunity to learn to play drums as he played drums for the "Soul Brothers Band". All these people are now with the Lord. They are really missed.

Lastly, I must thank Neo and TrubuPress for their support and faith in producing this book.

CONTENTS

TABLE OF CONTENTS

FOREWORD

Years ago as part of a group of young associate ministers, each of us was assigned by the pastor to oversee an outreach ministry in the church. I enjoyed working with the older folks so I headed up visitations to nursing homes on Sunday afternoons to bring the Gospel to the sick and shut in. We had a joyous time singing and visiting the residents who looked forward to our visits.

There was one fellow in the church named Brother Joe who headed up The Tract Team. His was a group of individuals who hit the street going door to door greeting people and putting in a good word for God. They weren't pushy. Often they would just knock and ask if there was anything they could pray about that day. It was amazing how such a simple question to be of service brought new families to church each Sunday and even more to Christ right in their doorway.

Brother Joe, was a humble man with a street background that he wasn't really proud of. But it was that

FOREWORD

same background that made folks in those neighborhoods pay attention when he and his team would visit. Because if God could change Brother Joe with his reputation, maybe God could change them too. He was the right man for the job.

The Tract Team would always leave beginner's Christian literature in the form of mini easy to read comic booklets called tracts that would give people a basic start to understanding faith and God. Many times a tract would be based upon a true life Christian testimony that people could relate to.

Brother Joe and his team were my heroes. They served in the trenches and faced more than many would choose. Likewise I have a great admiration for the work of author Frank J. Bradford who so candidly reveals the tracts of his drug addicted years as a testimony for those still suffering addiction and hope to those who may be tempted to try drugs, that Christ is The Answer to living a better life and that it is never too late to be renewed and set free by the loving grace of God.

For many, these series of articles bound into this single book volume may be too explicit. But for those who really need a wake up call, I encourage you to pass along these tracts written by a man who truly knows and is truly blessed to have been used by God to lead others away from the deadly path of addiction.

-Neo Blagness, Publisher

INTRODUCTION

was born and raised in Champaign-Urbana, IL. I am the youngest of four of my mother and father, Robert and Eola Bradford who migrated from Macon, Mississippi to Urbana, IL. My older siblings are Percy, my oldest brother of Milwaukee, WI, Lillie, my older sister of Urbana, IL and C.R., my other brother of Elgin, IL.

Education during the time of my parents, were few and far between. When people migrate from the south from working in the fields at a young age with very little education, was difficult to get a good paying job in a small city. That was a challenge alone.

My parents arrived in Champaign-Urbana, IL in or around 1948 when my oldest brother and sister were at a young age. My other brother was born in 1949. Then I came later in January of 1951. As years passed, I learned different things in life at a young age to have good social skills. When my mother had to do domestic work I was being taken care of mostly by my

INTRODUCTION

uncle Archie, who taught me carpentry and aunt Mary, who showed me motherly love while my mother was at work. I was their first son while they were practicing on getting their own someday, which they did.

When I got around the age of 9 or 10, I started to find myself wanting to do more things and play more sports. I played little league baseball, grade school basketball and on through high school. When I got to the ages of 12 through 14, I was interested in music to go along with my sports so I decided to try to play drums and flute.

As the year kept creeping on, my flute instructor and I thought we were in love and we had a baby boy at a young age of 15. My mother was upset that her parents made her give him to an adoption facility. We were only kids didn't even know ourselves yet but I would continue to father children.

In 1969, at the age of 18, I graduated from Centennial high school and wanted to follow my dream of being an architectural draftsman. I studied diligently to create a path for my future. As soon as I graduated, I enrolled at Eastern Illinois University College June 69 to June 71 to continue my architectural skills.

During my second year in college, I joined the fraternity, Alpha Phi Alpha following my brother. About four months later, I found myself hanging around with a group of friends where I started to drink, have sex with college girls and party late nights. I found myself

INTRODUCTION

partying more than studying. I had to drop out of the university and try to attend a junior college for a couple of semesters.

It didn't work out so, I went back to my hometown for six months, worked and played in my band at many different places. Drinking and sex followed again in my life which I fathered even more children.

In November of 1971- November of 1973 following my oldest brother's footsteps, I decided to go to the army at the age of 20. By being in the army it gave me many opportunities to improve myself and have discipline in my life. I got married in Germany at a young age and fathered a son while serving in the military and left with an honorable discharge.

From the years of January1974 to March of 1976, I worked as a new furniture delivery man until the company went out of business and still played in the band (which didn't work out, members started being late at shows).

I moved to Milwaukee, WI to get a better job opportunity with skills. I got a job as a welder in April 1976 with a company that made truck and car frames for GM, Ford and Chrysler. The company paid very good wages and I saved $100 per week in three different banks and still had money left to pay my mortgage and bills with my second wife. I had fathered another child outside of that marriage in 1978.

When the dreadful year of 1983 fell in my life,

INTRODUCTION

"Stages of Addiction" knocked at my door and I let it come into my life until January of 1995. The company closed its doors in 2005, moved all operations to Mexico.

This book tells you about my past then and I am telling you about my present now. I am here today because of the Lord, who has guided my steps all the way through my trials and tribulations. There was a reason why the Lord left me here today after going through two major cancer surgeries in 2007. I am now cancer free after radiation therapy in 2010. Whenever I get a chance to, I speak to younger men about getting their life together and staying healthy by seeing a doctor an also giving their lives to the Great Physician, Jesus Christ.

I am now playing the flute and drums for the Lord at three different churches. I go to church on Sundays with my wife at 8am at one church and at 10am to play at another church. On Saturday's we have morning church service at 11am and I play the drums for that service. We also have Tuesday night services at 6:30pm and I have bible study on Wednesday nights at 5pm.

All of these things that I am doing, I try to stay focused while trying to keep my photography business going also. Standing by my side with me through all of my situations is my wife, author and motivational speaker, P. Utley Bradford. We have been married

INTRODUCTION

since 2007, but known each other for a lifetime.

Focus, stay busy and stay away from drugs if you want to live a gracious life.

TRACTS OF MY YEARS
AN ADDICTION TESTIMONY

By Frank J. Bradford

———————

TRUBU PRESS
A Black Legacy Publishing Company

Cocaine

Syllabification: (co·caine)
Pronunciation: /ko-kan', ko'kan /

noun (plural cocaine)

A colorless or white crystalline narcotic alkaloid, extracted from coca leaves and used as a local anesthetic.

TRACT ONE

STAGES OF A DOPE ADDICT

The idea of saying: *"I can control this stuff or I just use it some-times socially"* I was only fool-ing myself in trying to cover my drug addiction the best way that I could. This is called *"true lies"* because at that time, in my mind, those lies were true.

I used to think that to have friend, one would have to socialize and do what oth-ers do to achieve that certain status among people, even if it takes the acts of drinking and drugs.

I began to pick my friends, carefully screening them to increase my social status. I thought that the friends that I picked were up my alley, and they were. The dark alley to what I called; *Social Drug* use.

This so called social drug I chose lasted hours af-ter hours, days after days, months after months to years after years. I didn't realize how sociable it and I had become. No more Family, BROKE, Hungry and could not be trusted. I was controlling it!! So I thought

With the need for more money to buy more drugs, I began to sell my personal items that I had worked so hard to get before I got involved with this social drug. By the time I got to this point, I already spent my weekly check on drugs, being sociable.

I ignored my rent payments, car notes, electric, gas, and food just to get another social hit.

I continued doing drugs socially for years and found myself living in abandoned buildings and cars without food and heat during cold winters. I started eating my dinners at Churches that handed out bags of food from their pantry, hot meals, loaves of bread and clothes to the needy and the homeless.

I was really controlling this stuff and I was doing it socially sometimes. Yeah! Right! I was a social outcast and it had controlled me for more than eight years. It had reduced me to a shell of a man with no back-bone to stand up for my pride or respect.

I was running and hiding from my brothers and other relatives. I put my mother through mental worries and then to sickness. My mother didn't know if I were dead or alive. I cut off communication lines for at least five years because I was too embarrassed to face my family.

Shame and stupid was written on my face and one day after being sociable for five days straight, I looked in the mirror and I saw -- NOTHING.

TRACT TWO
THE SIDE EFFECTS

You may find it hard to believe that I went through this self- affliction situation. So far I am only scratching the surface in sparing you all the not- so- nice details. But, if only you knew, this could happen to you or anyone in your family. It could even be your friends or maybe your associates that you work with each week.

This drug has changed many people from rich to poor and from poor to poorer. It goes through all ethnic backgrounds and different categories of life. It stems from politicians to welfare to the homeless. There are no boundaries with this social drug. It will make a person loose their true identity under it's control.

Through all of those years of using the social drug I have had to confront many different ordeals such as, almost getting shot in the back of my head, getting raided in after-hour smoke houses, going to jail, driving with suspended licenses and getting stopped, getting into fights over this so called social drug. Even going as far as trying to steal food which was all new to me.

All of the situations were new to me and very frightening experiences that I care not to go through again.

Believe me, each ordeal that was mentioned, has a long hard-core story behind it and all together they are long enough to span eight years or more. And once you start going down that dark alley, your whole life starts going down-hill from there.

You'll think it's fun at the beginning and then from there, it gets serious. It starts beginning to be a job, number one priority, got to have it everyday, anyway possible, can't function without it.

YOU USE IT AS:

A HANDICAP

YOU ARE IN DENIAL

YOU ARE STUPID

YOU ARE HOOKED ON IT.

I used to be on the streets late at night or early in the mornings walking around looking for another hit. Thinking of ways to cheat or beat someone out of money and or dope. I made plans to find a victim that looked dumber than me. The thing was, I was the dumber one because it never worked out. I was GREEN to them.

Males and females, with no discrimination, it makes no difference. It's in Control !! It makes you want more and do things that you would never do in your right mind. So, if your mind is weak and easily influenced, don't step into the fire.

Don't let the side-effects of this social drug disrupt your life. Focus on a good future for yourself and your family. And most of all, focus on GOD because HE will get you through all the ordeals that you will face in your entire life.

TRACT THREE

A BULLET WITH NO NAME

There are reasons why I continue to write about drugs. One is to get it off of my chest which is a burden and the other is, to get it off someone else's mind before it sticks there and lead to addiction. If I could just change one person's thoughts or habit I would feel that my articles were not written in vain.

I have chosen to write about one of my ordeals in depth to give you some kind of insight on what this drug and it's power can do to anyone without notice.

It was a cool early summer evening and I was driving my car almost on empty. I needed to buy gas and had no money. I decided to try renting my services out as a driver taking dope dealer's to pick up drugs. This way, I could get a few dollars for gas and drugs too.

I had picked up two drug dealer's whom I thought were good people and used to purchase my drugs from. One of them asked me to take them to pick up a large package so they could break it down for the sale on the streets. At the time, it sounded good until they told me how far away it was and I had a suspended drivers license.

One was in the front passengers seat and the other was in the rear passengers side. As I was explaining to the one in the front that I had no drivers license to be going that far, the one in the rear butted in and said, " YOU ARE GOING TO TAKE US TO GET THE STUFF ". And as I turned around, there was a gun pointed at my face. I was taken by surprise and with the fear of dying, I pushed the gun over with my left hand and POW! the gun went off, leaving powder burns on my wrist and forehead. The bullet went through the front windshield. The bullet had no name on it--at that time--but it was meant for me. I do think it had my name on it, but GOD took it off.

They both got out and ran as I staggered out of the car dazed seeing my whole life flash before my very eyes. I saw myself lying on a stainless steel table being cut open for an autopsy, my family standing over me in my coffin and myself being covered with dirt. Not being able to see my family anymore was the shocker.

That day was a complete learning lesson of the streets that would normally take years to absorb, took only a few minutes for me, in front of a gun with a bullet with no name. I could have been just another statistic in the obituary pages in the newspaper.

I THANK GOD ! for looking over me and giving me another chance at life -- a good life.

Thank you, JESUS !

This is straight from my heart, DON'T BE AN-OTHER STATISTIC young or old and remember always that : BULLETS HAVE NO NAMES.

Being hooked on drugs will cause a person to do things that they would not normally do. I should have been at work at that time anyways. I just wanted an-other hit, which it almost caused me to lose my life.

TRACT FOUR
MURDER ONE

The thought of having the police close off a two block radius with unmarked and marked cars, trucks, patty wagons and even foot patrol policemen closing in on me was an eerie feeling. They had closed in so quietly I could hear a pin drop on the floor.

While a so-called friend and I were watching television in the dark after getting our "social drug" hit, the next thing I knew, bright beams of light from flashlights were blinding us. With rifles and pistols drawn a loud deep voice shouted out "DON'T MOVE! - GET YOUR HANDS UP AND GET ON THE FLOOR!".

I didn't have a clue to whom they were looking for.

While they were surrounding us with precision tactics, I heard other voices on their radios crackle with the sound of static, one officer asked, "WHAT ARE YOUR NAMES?"

The other guy answered with his name first and when I said my name, the police quickly spoke into his radio and said, "WE"VE GOT HIM!".

They had put handcuffs on me without letting me tie my boots or put on my jacket. I nicely asked "why am I being arrested?"

An officer replied "MURDER ONE LET'S GO!"

It was very cold that night in the month of January with the wind chills of twenty below zero. I quickly replied "I did not kill anyone".

The police officer said "WE WILL TALK ABOUT THIS DOWNTOWN".

With two officers on both sides of me and my hands cuffed behind my back, they lead me down the stairs to a waiting police wagon to transport me to jail. All I could say was "you've got the wrong man and I am innocent".

They did not want to hear it. They said they had been looking for me for a week and all the places that I had been, they had just missed me by a few minutes.

The only thing they really told me was that I'd better find a good lawyer, because I will need one. While in the back of the wagon going to the downtown station, I kept asking myself, why me? I didn't kill anyone.

Before I got to the downtown jail, the police had picked up three other people to join me in rear of the wagon. A conversation had started in why were we incarcerated. One guy said, "domestic violence" another said, "drunk driving". The last guy asked me, -why were you arrested? I replied, "MURDER ONE" and suddenly a chill came in the air and froze all conversations during the rest of the ride to jail.

When we arrived at the jail, the police herded us out of the back of the wagon like cattle and into the station to be processed in to our holding cells. They stripped me of all of my personal belongings from head to toe and gave me their bright orange uniform with COUNTY JAIL written on the back and a pair of thong flipper shoes. They also took my picture and fingerprinted me.

I was marked as a murderer, which entitled me to a 5 by 7 foot cell of my own. A stainless steel bed, a stainless steel toilet/face bowl combination and bars on my door for a view. No windows, no radio, no comforts of a home -- only silence -- which was so quiet, I could hear my heart beat and my pulse racing through my veins.

Darkness loomed inside my cell where only the light that I could see came from the hallway through the bars and at the bottom of the door. When I called for an officer or coughed, I could hear echoes bounce off of the walls. Time was all I had to contend with and I had become to realized that being in jail, was nothing but time.

During my three day stay in jail I was interrogated two days about three a.m. to six a.m. and then returned to my cell. And on the third day, they found evidence that I did not commit the crime and released me at four in the morning. This was a time when the buses stop running and I had no money for a taxi, therefore, I had to walk.

I was a free man and I didn't mind the walk because, I could have been in there for the rest of my life tagged with "MURDER ONE" and innocent. FIRST DEGREE HOMICIDE was a big charge to carry on my back when I knew I didn't do it.

The only good thing about it even though I wasn't aware at the time was that I was not walking alone. GOD walked with me through it all. I thank the LORD everyday simply because HE was there with me throughout this ordeal and saw fit to bring the truth to light.

TRACT FIVE

THE REASON

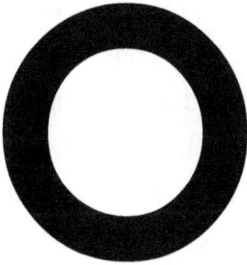

One would wonder why I was arrested for murder one after reading my last article. I purposely left it out because I wanted to tell my experiences from this ordeal from the beginning. I want to let people know that jail is no joke and I could have been also charged for drug possession if the police had only looked around for it. Murder one and drug possession, think about it.

If I could just stop one person from being in this "social drug" situation , I would feel that my mission to stop them from going down that spiral staircase would be a success.

As I see it, all of my ordeals stems from the usage of this "social drug" to where the "Reason" comes into the picture. I was being charged for murder one because of a dead body that was found stuffed in a closet where I had my bag of clothes, and a travel bag with my ID, and my mother's name, address and telephone number.

It was about two thirty a.m. in the morning, still dark and cold with snow about seven inches deep. I just had purchased a couple of rocks and was on my way to the house that I was allowed to stay in for "social drug" hits or a rock. As I was walking towards the door. I looked down at the snow and saw all types of foot-prints entering and leaving from the door.

The friend that lived in the house had told me that the back door will be unlocked and to walk right on in. As I walked into the door which leads through the kitchen. it was very dark and quiet. There's normally a small light on that you could see as you stand in the kitchen but, there was no light on this time. Complete darkness. I couldn't even see my hand in front of my face.

The hair on the back of my neck started moving. It was an eerie feeling. It felt as though there was a presence in the air. And with the first thought of my mind saying, "leave". I did just that.

At that time, I was thinking of only myself for safety. I kept thinking that someone was there in the darkness waiting to shoot me or hit me with something. So, I quickly backed out of the door and headed to the place where I was arrested four days later.

Little did I know that the Milwaukee police had gotten all of the information from my bags and called my mother looking for me. At that time, I had not seen my mother in three years. That call made her worry and think that I was dead because the police had found my bags covered with blood and no sign of me. It was only because they kept missing me by a few minutes and that's why I had not been picked up before that day.

What I found out was that, it was my friend that let me stay there, was tied up, strangled with their throat cut and marks all over the body from beatings. All because of the so-called "social drug" that was fronted to sell for the person and never was because the victim was the only customer. It was smoked up before it was sold. The person that did it knew the victim was hooked and took a chance anyways. If it had not been for the other persons skin under the victims fingernails and the grace of GOD, I would not be here today to write about all of my ordeals.

Remember: only YOU can stop yourself from going through all of these ordeals that affect more people than you would ever think by doing this "social drug". Most important of all, you hurt yourself internally and externally.

I want to thank the LORD again, for giving me the strength to rise above.

TRACT SIX

THE SMOKEHOUSE RAID

wondered many times now, why did I let myself go through all of these ordeals with the use of the "social drug". The thing is that; it controls every nerve cell that goes to your brain which makes you do its bidding.

It also makes you want more and more and yet, you still won't achieve the pinnacle with the usage.

This is what most addicts call, "chasing a ghost". It makes you stay out in all types of weather and times. It makes you walk or drive to certain high crime areas where you know that the drug is abundant.

With this in mind, come take a walk with me to a drug smokehouse through the power of reading. Remember, we must go purchase the drug and make it back without getting caught by the police.

We are down to our last funds. You and I have five dollars each and we combine our assets to purchase a ten dollar rock half the size of a mini marsh mallow. The only bad thing about it is, we have to walk about ten long blocks to get it. It is three a.m. rainy and cool. We both must go because we don't really trust each other due to the fact that whomever picks it up would take a piece off and put it in his pocket. This way, when we both come out it would be broken evenly on the spot.

But, this night was different, I was primed up. My mind is thinking of how I can get more than you from this bag so, I say to you " Why don't you let me go get this by myself. I can get it and be back in a shorter amount of time than two going to get it."

And you agree to this because of the bad weather.

As I was walking to the drug house I kept imagining myself taking that "social drug" hit all alone without other people asking me for a hit. I was thinking to myself that I can get the stuff as quickly as I could - an in and out thing. Come out, go around the back and take a hit for the walk back.

I walked through the back pathway that had two large hedges on both sides and broken pieces of concrete off of the sidewalk. As I stumbled in the dark to the steps from the loose concrete pieces, I made it up to the door and knocked. A minute later the mail slot cover opens with a screech, then a voice said " WHAT DO YOU WANT ? "

I replied "a dime".

The unknown voice spoke again, "MOVE TO THE MIDDLE OF THE DOOR SO I CAN SEE YOUR FACE ".

After the frontal view, the cover closes and then the door begins it's opening with the sounds of dead bolts unlocking and a large three by three board that crosses the door horizontally near the door knob. As the door opens, the person said "COME ON IN".

I stepped in and gave the guy my money as he closes and locks the door. I started looking around from that very spot that I stood and noticed that the place looked just like NEW JACK CITY.

I gazed to my left, I saw people drinking and snorting cocaine at a makeshift cocktail table. I looked straight ahead and saw people smoking cocaine sitting on a legless old torn couch. And as I started to look to my right, -BOOM!! the door was knocked loose from the hinges and laid on the floor next to me.

Within a second, black uniforms with black chest protectors, black masks and weapons drawn in a ready to shoot stance was in on us. At least five loud voices shouted "EVERYBODY ON THE FLOOR!! DON'T MOVE!! AND DON'T LOOK UP!"

There was at least twenty-five law enforcement agents. It was a raid. The law, drug and enforcement team had came in with precise timing and team work that no one had time enough to do any hiding of the drugs or paraphernalia.

From what I saw, there were about sixty people face down on the floor, males and females including myself. We all were handcuffed with thick plastic strips bands with our hands behind our backs.

The enforcement team set up their post right there on the spot and processed people out one by one. One agent shouted "IF YOU DON'T HAVE AN WISCONSIN ID OR DRIVERS LICENSE, YOU ARE GOING TO JAIL!"

Luckily, I had an ID and after going in the smokehouse when it was dark, it was daylight when I was finally fingerprinted and processed. I stepped out of the other door, the sun was so bright my eyes could not adjust. It was like being in total darkness for six hours, and then coming out into an instant bright light.

What I thought it was going to be an in and out purchase ended up as an all nighter with nothing to go back with. Broke and Hungry. No Drugs. Only just another charge on my record at the police station and a two-hundred and eighty dollar ticket for being in the "SMOKEHOUSE RAID".

I thank the LORD for being there with me to make it through this ordeal because they could have came in shooting and ask the questions later.

Thank you JESUS!!

TRACT SEVEN
THE GETAWAY DRIVER

n my last article, I had encountered the police through a smokehouse raid. Within a few months later my driver's license was taken due to non-payment of tickets that I got during the raid. The next ordeal involved driving the get-a-way car for liquor thieves.

With what money I was suppose to have gotten from them, I would have spent it on that "social drug" not caring about paying the tickets, gas or anything that matters for correcting the mess that I was making. This leads into the one ordeal that took place as the get-a-way driver during the time when I used the "social drug".

I was asked by two so-called friends to take them on the south side of the city so that they could pick up their checks. I was low on gas and wanted another hit, so I agreed to do it.

There I was, with STUPID written on my face, driving without license.

During the long ride to the south side of the city I was asked to pulled up by the door of a food and liquor store and just wait there until they go in to get their checks. They were in there for about five or six minutes and I had began to wonder what was taking them so long.

As I looked back at the door, one of them was coming out of the store and he got in the front seat and said "go ahead and start the car, he'll be right out" and I did just that. As I looked back through the rear window of the car to see if the other guy was coming out, I saw him hurrying out with a fast pace.

Quickly the other guy jumped in the back seat and closed the car door, I heard the words, "Take Off!, Take Off!!".

I was stunned in what I saw. There was a worker and a security guard running out of the store chasing me on foot getting my license plate number off of my car as I drove off. I shouted, "what did you two do?" The next thing I knew, they were pulling large bottles of liquor out of their pants and coats then started putting them on the floor of the car.

I looked at them with the meanest face and said "you two have to get this stuff out of my car right now". I pulled over to a side street for them to take the liquor out of the car and they threw the bottles behind some bushes.

Suddenly I heard police sirens coming from all directions. I drove for about four blocks from where they threw the bottles out and then we were stopped.

The police had surrounded us within three minutes. They jumped out of the cars with their guns drawn and rushed to all of the doors of my car. One officer said " PUT YOUR HANDS ON THE DASHBOARD AND SLOWLY GET YOUR DRIVER'S LICENSE OUT " - (I had none)

After fumbling around in my wallet for about three minutes, I tried faking as though I left them at home on my dresser. The officer stated "IF YOU DON'T HAVE NO DRIVER'S LICENSE YOU ARE GOING TO JAIL".

He then asked " WHAT IS YOUR NAME? "

I told him my name.

As I looked around there were about ten police officers pointing high powered rifles, shotguns and pistols at the windows, the full circumference of the car.

The one officer quickly said "STAY RIGHT HERE " then walked back to his squad car called in my name on the radio to the main station, then entered it into the computers inside the car and found that my driver's licenses were suspended, I had unpaid tickets from previous arrests and I was also fined for driving the get-a-way car in the aiding of the thefts as a party to the crime that has just been committed.

There I was, being handcuffed again with another ride down to the police station in the back of a patty wagon and with more charges added on to my record as a criminal.

Whenever someone talk about a spiral staircase downward, this is exactly the way your life goes when you decide to use the "social drug". Once one bad thing goes wrong and then from there, it is all downhill like a domino effect. It will be one bad ordeal after another which will plague you like a disease. You will not have a good life using this mind altering drug. Once you get started there is no turning back unless you help yourself or get some type of counseling.

There is a lesson behind all of this: make sure that you have real friends and know where or if they really work. Most of all, don't let this "social drug" take control of your senses. Stay away from its clutches!!

TRACT EIGHT

HOMELESS

am beginning to wonder now that I have changed my life, if I had stayed on that "social drug", what would I be like today? It is a scary thought. I never knew how precious life was until I decided to cross over onto the world of drugs. There are things that I never thought that I would do just to continue its use.

I had lost all respect for the words: hygiene and clean clothes. The main reason was because I would spend every penny that I could put my hands on. I would think that if I didn't pay rent, didn't pay utilities, didn't buy food, didn't buy soap or didn't wash my clothes, there would be more money for me to purchase a larger quantity of drugs.

The stupid thing was, I did just that- not a care in the world, until, I was broke. Afterwards, I would start to worry about how I am going to pay rent and then I would feel like a fool. I would swear to myself that I would not do that again. YEAH!, RIGHT!

That little guilt trip only lasted long enough until I got my hands on more money.

By me not paying my bills, a few months later I found myself with an eviction notice with police escorts. I had resorted to living on the streets, walking up and down alleys rummaging through garbage cans looking for aluminum cans or any useful item that I could turn in for cash at the recycling center.

There I was, a few months later being a semi-professional scavenger with a food store grocery cart full of aluminum cans and a somewhat working twelve inch black and white TV. that I had found walking up and down alleys for hours digging in garbage dumpsters that hosted a family of maggots that lived on spoiled meats and dead rats.

The smell alone was enough to make any stomach turn to vomit but, I was determined to continue until I bagged up to a certain amount of pounds of cans to get twenty dollars. Ten for a rock, a pack of cigarettes and a fifth of MD 20/20. I was HAPPY --- THEN --- which only lasted a few minutes. No more than five minutes. The rock was gone, the wine was gone and I was back to square one again.

The only thing that was left for me to do was take my cart with my little TV, find a church that gives hot meals, or a bag of food donations, and go find myself a spot in the abandoned building to go to sleep. There were other people that lived in the building and they had their own law as squatters. They were there first and that abandon room was their domain. If you had a rock, they would want you to stay there with them, until it was gone. Then you would have to go so there would be an opening for another person with a rock.

These people were very serious about their living quarters. They took pride in their vacant run-down , rat infested during the summer and winter, along with heavy roach infestation in the summer abode. There were no working toilets or bathtubs. Both had fallen plaster from the ceiling and walls on the inside. The toilet was the worst. It was full to the rim with plaster, feces and newspaper where you can hear the wings of flies buzzing all night. There wasn't any view outdoors because the windows were covered with boards.

My bed was made of cushion from a sofa that someone had thrown out in the trash. This was an improvement compared to using old clothes laid out on the floor. Zippers and buttons make bad mattresses, but it worked. This prevented the coldness of the floor to get to my body. I also used clothes on top of me as a blanket. This was a step higher than sleeping in an abandon car during the cold weather at nights.

Why I chose to live like this is way beyond my imagination to answer. Maybe in one of my up-coming articles I will have figured it out through my writings of this self-therapy-counseling program. I'm only hoping that what I write, through my eyes of experience will one day change the course of action that someone may take toward this "social drug".

Being homeless is not fun. It is very dangerous. You will never know who's lurking in the dark of an abandon building or in the alleys. There is a fifty percent chance that you will survive this dilemma and be able to discuss it among family and friends. The other, maybe your demise.

Again, I thank the LORD for giving me the best fifty I ever had. --- LIFE ---

TRACT NINE
NO SHAME IN MY GAME

There must be some kind of numbness that impales your body whenever the use of the "social drug" has been over a few years. It seemed to control every fiber of my being. The things that I did for another hit of that "social drug" was very uncommon to my norms of living. I had resorted to the beg, borrow or steal theory. The stealing part took more nerves than brains.

On two different occasions, I tried the act of stealing and both times I came up empty handed. One incident was on the third birthday of one of my children.

After I had spent all of my check on the "social drug" that I had been doing since early noon, I was supposed to have purchased a birthday cake for his party. I had the money in my hands and yet it burned like a hot potato.

Something in my mind kept saying "GO ON ! -- JUST ONE MORE -- ONE MORE DIME WON'T HURT!!!"

That one more dime ended up to be ten which caused me to go broke four hours later. No money! No birthday cake! No pride! Only stupidity and guilt was written all over my face. I hung my head down as though I had lost my right to live.

Now, I was desperately in the need of a cake. That little voice came to me again, "WHY NOT GO TO THE STORE AND GRAB ONE AND WALK OUT OF THE DOOR?"

I was already primed up from the "social drug" and it didn't take much for me to follow that voice. So, I walked into a grocery store and walked around like I was shopping, (not knowing I was being watched). I headed towards the cakes that were close to the exit door. I looked around and picked one as though I was interested in the flavor or toppings. I kept looking down at the cake and then at the exit door. (I didn't know I was still being watched).

I finally built up my nerves. I headed towards the door with the cake in my hands and I was only a few steps to the exit door, suddenly a big security guard stepped in front of me and said, "HEY! YOU DIDN'T PAY FOR THAT CAKE!!".

I shoved it in his hands and ran out of the store. I didn't want to face the police again at that time. I was back to square one again, still in need of a cake for my son's birthday. I should have just purchased the cake at first to avoid the guilt trip.

Oh! Nooo! I couldn't do that, I had to get my "social drug" hit before bills or family. I owed this to myself for working that day. -- Stupidity Steps In -- I gave myself a gift and a pat on the back. Neither of the two were good gestures. It was all just for the drugs.

The other occasion, was two an a half years earlier and I had spent all of my money that night. That morning during one of my "social drug" hits, I realized there was no baby formula for another of my children. He was crying and hungry. The only thing that I could think of doing is to go to the store and try to steal it. It was cold and I had to walk at least eight blocks in the snow.

As I walked into the store, I saw it was quite busy and I started thinking that this was just the right time to make my move. So, I walked to the back of the store where the meats were and said to myself, I should grab a package of meat for me.

That voice blurted out again, "GO AHEAD, GRAB A PACK OF BOLOGNA --IT"S SMALL -- and then GO GET THE CAN OF FORMULA, PUT THEM IN-SIDE YOUR COAT -- GO TO THE CASH REGIS-TER WITH AN ITEM THAT COST A QUARTER AND THEN OUT OF THE DOOR YOU GO".

Little that I know, I was not walking out of the door by myself. There were three plain clothes workers that followed me out and stopped me right on the lot and said to me "COME BACK INTO THE STORE WITH US".

They took me to the office and told me that "WE HAVE BEEN WATCHING YOU THROUGH THE CAMERA". They said to me, "EMPTY YOUR POCKETS". I did just that and their mouths flew opened after they saw I only had a can of formula and a package of bologna.

One guard said "I THOUGHT THAT YOU WERE TAKING STEAKS, CHOPS AND ROASTS. THIS DOES NOT COST ENOUGH TO CALL THE PO-LICE, BUT WHAT WE WILL DO IS GIVE YOU THE MILK FOR THE BABY AND NOT THE BO-LOGNA, YOU FIND YOURSELF SOMEWHERE TO EAT AND DON'T COME BACK INTO THIS STORE AGAIN".

I had came to a realization that I had no shame in my so-called game. I went through all of these ordeals without any sense of pride or respect for myself as a human being. I had no shame because I let the "social drug" control my thoughts and ruin my life.

TRACT TEN
THE CHANGING OF MY MIND

Drugs, alcohol or cigarettes it makes no difference. They all have the control over every part of you when your body wants more. They all make you urge for another hit or drink. There is no escape unless you make changes in your life.

There were many times that I thought that I had control over the so called "social drug". Each time that I got a chance I would spend all of my money and later I would feel guilty. I would be hard on myself and say the words out loud, "I am through with this stuff". No sooner than I got more money from anywhere that I could, there I was, going to the dealer looking for another hit.

Anytime that I would go to get another hit, there would be two or three people sitting there that would start asking for a piece or a hit. They all would have some type of reason to ask for it. One would say, "DO YOU REMEMBER WHEN?" Another would say,

"DON'T YOU OWE ME ?" or the other would say "I'LL RETURN THE FAVOR AS SOON AS .... ".

And if you would fall for it like I did, you would end up back to square one again within four minutes, especially when you only buy just one little small rock.

One should learn from the ordeals of the "social drug" but, that faint echo sound inside your head seems to tell your mind that it's not finished.

GET MORE! THINK! WHERE CAN YOU GET MORE MONEY? MAYBE YOU SHOULD SELL SOMETHING THAT YOU OWN OR SOMEONE ELSE OWNS? THINK! THINK! THINK!

There is an old saying "think long and you will think wrong." This rule comes into affect when you hear that little voice. Don't be weak. Stand strong. Don't fall into its clutches.

You must remember that you are not alone. There is SOMEONE there with you all of the time. Ask for help. Don't be ashamed to let SOMEONE know that you need guidance to the correct path. Only you, can change the out-come of your life with the help of the LORD.

I thank HIM everyday for waking me up, for being able to be mobile and for having a sound mind to be able to write these words through all of my ordeals and experiences. Living through these ordeals and being able to talk about it is a blessing in itself. The ordeals that I have faced and survived, GOD made it possible for me to relay these messages to all of you that have or may decide to use this "social drug."

GOD is the number one reason for the changing of my mind and along with the strong desire to retrieve my life is the other. I refuse to hear that little echoing voice because I know that it's wrong and what it can do to me. It would put me back through all of those ordeals again and I might not survive the next trauma.

Thank you JESUS for being there to pick me up when I was down.

I now have the strength to walk through the church doors with my head held high and pray to HIM for letting me see a better life for myself.

TRACT ELEVEN

FAMILY VALUES

The more I think about it, I believe that if it were not for my desire to change and GOD'S GRACE, I would not be here today to write the perils that I had experienced during my involvement with the "social drug".

Throughout all of those years, I had lost all sense of feelings for holidays and birthdays because I was around people that didn't care about neither of those days. The truth is, I was always broke. If I were to have bought gifts it would cut in on the amount of the "social drug" that I could purchase. As I analyze myself, then, if I had any money for presents, it would have been spent on the "social drugs" as a gift to myself.

I often wondered, while I was on the streets how and what my mother and family were doing on the holidays. I was too ashamed to face them in my condition. I had lost weight, my clothes were dirty and my personal hygiene wasn't far from a skunk.

I remember looking in a mirror and seeing a reflection of me as the skull and bones of death. My face was drawn in as though there was a high powered vacuum suction inside of my head. My clothes had not been washed in weeks. I just couldn't let my family see me in this state of mind and the bad living conditions.

My family knew that I used to live a better life than that and they could not see how I got into this turmoil in the first place. It's easy when you decide to go to the drug side of life. There was nothing they could do for me except give me moral support and that's just what I needed along with the grace of GOD to combat the powerful grip that the "social drug" had on me.

I took more time out for the "social drug" than I did trying to clean myself up and enjoy my real family. Friends were alright but, family is more important than anyone could imagine when it comes to sharing holidays or birthdays when you're trying to rehabilitate yourself. Through the years of my involvement with the "social drug", I had became numb to any special day due to the fact that the drug was more important to me than breathing oxygen.

For many years I did not know how to get out of the situation that I put myself into. I was running around like a chicken with it's head cut off. I had no direction or goals implanted in my mind to even begin to correct my horrid lifestyles.

There were many factors in getting the help that I needed to put me on the road to recovery. Believe me, I didn't do this all on my own. The main thing is that, I wanted to change the way I was living.

I prayed and asked GOD to help me change that horrible looking man that was in the mirror. With the help of my family through understanding and tough love, I was able to overcome the handicap in the use of the drugs.

Since I had the moral support from my family and real friends, I have regained my dignity, pride and self-respect. I feel like a human being again and I feel there is nothing that can stop me from being the best that I can be.

I finally woke up to reality and realized that family values are very important assets to the mental well-being of an addict that wants to recover from the many ordeals of it's use.

I still thank the LORD everyday for giving me the opportunity to be able to spend valuable time with my family and real friends.

TRACT TWELVE

TOUGH LOVE

AMILY. This is a word that is meant to be a strong binding factor in anyone's life. If it were not for family bonding and a willing to change all would be lost in the crusade to kick any habit. Moral support had a big role in my "social drug" dramatic experiences which I care not to go through anymore in my lifetime.

My family and real friends were there hoping that one day they could see me come to my senses before I lost them for good. Tough love is the best thing that a family member could give to an addict when it comes to any form of drug.

This brings into mind of an ordeal where my oldest brother gave me the toughest love ever, that later opened my eyes and which is etched into my mind still today.

It all started the days I refused to admit that I had a problem. I would get paid on Thursday evenings and after I would get off of work I would go purchase a quantity of rocks. Then, I would go find a place to smoke it, like a so-called friends home.

I would be there for two to three days sending other people to buy more when I ran out of what I had purchased. One day, my brother was looking for me to see if I was alright since I was away from my home for days. He happened to see my car parked out in front of my so-called friends home and knocked on the door.

KNOCK!- KNOCK!

I was in the process of getting my high on. My so-called friend call to me in the other room and said "YOUR BROTHER IS AT THE DOOR!".

I replied, "I AM NOT HERE!"

Stupid me, my car was out doors in the front. The next thing I knew, he was standing in the doorway of the room that I was in and with red fire in his eyes and the meanest look I have ever seen and said "GET THE H--- OUT OF THIS HOUSE RIGHT NOW! AND IF I SEE YOU HERE AGAIN, I WILL BEAT YOU DOWN AND CALL THE POLICE ON EVERY-BODY IN HERE AND THEN I WILL CALL MOM TELL HER WHAT YOU ARE DOING AND WHERE YOU WILL BE - IN JAIL> GET THE H...--- OUT OF HERE RIGHT NOW!"

My so-called friend turned to me and said "YOU BETTER LEAVE BECAUSE I DON'T WANT THE POLICE UP IN HERE!"

So, I left only to find myself all that day with a paranoid state of mind. Even when I searched and found other places to go, I was paranoid. I would start looking and peeping out of the windows every time I would take a hit of that "social drug", thinking that my brother would be driving around and walk up to the door and KNOCK. I couldn't enjoy the "social drug" anymore.

(TOO PARANOID)

The next time I saw my brother he brought what little articles that I had to me and said "I DON'T WANT YOU AROUND ME OR MY FAMILY UNTIL YOU GET YOUR LIFE STRAIGHT. ALL I WANT TO KNOW OF YOU IS THAT YOU ARE STILL ALIVE."

I stood there with my mouth opened wide as though my heart was about to come out of it and drop on the ground. Was it love or the hate of me using? The Answer-- Both of them.

It was a form of tough love which I needed for the realization to family moral support.

I thank the LORD for letting me keep my sanity to know the difference.

Hey!   You out there!   Wake up!   Life is short, don't misuse or abuse it.

TRACT THIRTEEN
VESSEL OF HONOR

know by now, that all of you are wondering how I can continue to write the articles of my true life experiences. Well, to tell you how I do it, it goes as far back as fifteen years from the year of nineteen hundred and ninety-five. All of the things that I had done were all experiments that transpired into a habit. I never saw it coming and I never realized that I had a problem with the "social drug" after all of those years of usage.

When January thirtieth of two thousand and two arrived on my birthday, I was clean for six years and proud of it. I had given myself a birthday present on that day. (A new lease on life along with the Grace of GOD.)

I wanted to change the horrible man that I had seen in the mirror. No other person, but me, could change that skin and bones man that reflected from within of the horrid lifestyles of an addict. The ordeals that I write as articles are therapeutic. It helps me keep the "social drug" thoughts at bay. I don't need it nor miss using it, because GOD is giving me a natural high.

I wake up everyday able to breathe and able to be mobile. All I need is for the sun to rise, live another day and be satisfied that there is another day to thank GOD for. I am free to come and go as I please to do the things that HE wants me to do. I am only HIS vessel. The LORD may use me anyway that HE feels.

This brings back to mind, an ordeal in one of my past articles when I was incarcerated and was being charged for first degree homicide.

There was no freedom within my mind nor my body. I thought that I was all alone but, the LORD was there with me all of the time and HE set the records straight. I was innocent. They had the wrong person and a few days later I was freed. Again, I thank the LORD for standing beside me through that terrible ordeal.

One never knows how precious life and freedom is until you go behind the bars. You are helpless and reduced to being a human in a cage, like a mad dog ready to be put down as though you have rabies. All of your personal items that you have in your possession are taken from you. You are searched from head to toe as though you were going to be sold on an auction block It is a bad feeling to be walking around with handcuffs and chains as jewelry.

The bad thing about it, the ordeals that I faced all derived from using that "social drug" and the strange thing is that: It doesn't discriminate. It sees no color, ethnic background nor social status.

When you decide to take a chance on playing with the white stuff, you might as well play Russian Roulette.

I searched deep within me to the depths of my intelligence and asked the LORD to help me overcome the powerful grip that this "social drug" had on me. I faced my problems head on and I accepted the fact that: "I can do all things through CHRIST which strengthened me." (Philippians' 4:13)

I feel today that, the LORD saved me for a reason. It is to try and change someone's mind from getting caught up in the "social drug" usage. If I can just stop one person from thinking the thoughts of, "ONE TIME WON'T HURT", "I'VE GOT IT UNDER CONTROL" or "I ONLY DO IT SOCIALLY, ONCE IN A WHILE", I will have done the job that HE wants me to do. I am HIS vessel which I honor and I am proud to be one for HIM.

Listen Up Addicts! Find something deep within yourself that you can do to improve your life. Think of something that you are good at and that can benefit you. Put your money to good use. You know that you like money. Why give your hard earned money away to a drug dealer? You can't get any credit from him when you have spent all of your earnings with him. Your pockets are empty, not one red cent. You are broke, left without food, no money to pay the rent and then you start hiding from the landlord with no bills paid. Then there you are, on the outside looking in. Nowhere to go or nothing to do, you are lost in the world of the "social drug".

There is no honor among drug addicts but, there is with the LORD. Thank you JESUS for letting me be YOUR vessel which I honor to the depths of my heart and soul.

TRACT FOURTEEN

AMAZING IN HIS GRACE

When it comes to asking for forgiveness from the LORD, your mind and body must go through some changes. You MUST be at HIS mercy.

There is no half stepping what-so-ever. It is all or nothing at all. The way I see it, the more you praise HIM, the more the blessings come down. They may not be there when you want them to be but, they are there right on time.

I was blessed on Memorial Day 2001. I was asked to play my flute at a cemetery in Champaign, IL for the father of a very close friend of mine. He passed away about 3yrs ago and was a Veteran of WWII. The grave site was for the fallen soldiers of the United States military.

I was very honored to be asked to play my flute over his grave site. The family of the fallen one were there with flowers and heavy hearts. There were also other families that placed flowers on their loved ones site. The thing that made me feel even more honored was that my mother was there also to listen and watch as I put my flute to my lips as I started to play.

They all bowed there heads as though they were speaking in silence to the spirit that was beneath their heals. Somehow, I felt it in the song that I played which in my heartbeat counted the tempo of the speed of the music.

There was silence in the air. It was so quiet, that one could hear a pin drop upon the grass. After I finished the song, one HONOR GUARD walked up to me and asked if I would play that song again for all of the fallen Soldiers of all of the Wars along with a 21 gun salute. I was blessed even more. It was only meant for one that I played for, which turn into playing for hundreds of military soldiers that lost their lives for the United States.

As I played that song, I kept thinking that I could have been in one of those grave sites and someone else could have been playing that song over me if I had continued to indulge with the "social drug". GOD had saved a wretch like me even when I was blinded to the uses of the controlling substance of cocaine.

I was lost in the dreadful world of sin and with HIS blessings I found that I can now see. AMEN! That social drug could have taken what little senses that were left within me and put me to rest without my knowledge.

The graces of GOD are super strong because if it had not been for HIM, I would not be here today. The sweet sounds of the notes that I played with my flute ascended in the air yet could not be seen is like the soul that would leave you when you sit down at the table for your last hit.

It's all over. No more heartbeats, no more air to breathe, no more blood circulating through your veins; you are finished. You might get some bad stuff, the kind that leaves you stiff with your eyes wide open to see your demise.

It is amazing what the LORD can do for you or anyone if you just let HIM do HIS work. There is no limit to HIS graces or blessing. HE has blessed me to be able to continue to play my flute and write all that I remember of my ordeals even after all of the things I went through. I think HE wants me to pass my bad ordeals along to stop whomever is on the "social drug", alcohol or whatever the habit is.

I thank the LORD for HIS graces that HE gave to me, I was blessed to be able to play the song

" AMAZING GRACE ".

HOW SWEET THE SOUND! I WAS LOST AND NOW I"M FOUND.

Thank you JESUS!

TRACT FIFTEEN
A NEW BEGINNING

magine it! A little white powder that sparkles with any beam of light, even with the moon or the stars. It looks so innocent but yet is so deadly to your mind and body.

This is a drug that you will spend your last dollar on and it will make you sell, beg, borrow or steal. The little white powder that will take control of your brain cells, take control of the rhythm of your heart beat and pollutes your blood stream with chemicals throughout your entire body. It leaves no cell unturned.

This "social drug" will ROCK your world. No matter what status you are in life, it will destroy and break you down to a mere shell of a person. I know because it broke me down and even other people that were in higher status than myself. It has gotten to governors, senators, movie stars, policemen and star athletes. You name it, its been there and done that. For you who have survived any ordeal with the use of the "social drug", you should thank the LORD for letting you live to see another day. I thank HIM for all of the things that he has done for me and everyone in this world.

Since the LORD is using me as a vessel to spread the word, "Don't Use Drugs" it has made me feel more at ease dealing with my past habits. I feel really good about the way my life has changed for the best since I gave myself to the LORD.

All of the bad troubles I had in the past, I don't have anymore. I found out there is a better way to live than on the edge in the streets and doing that so called "social drug".

This brings into mind a special day that filled my heart with a spirit of joy. A holy moment that chased away all evil thoughts from my mind completely. It was a proud moment which I held my head high and feeling fully blessed.

I was baptized. That special day was on September 9, 2001. A day that will forever be etched into my mind and heart. It was a wonderful feeling that made me feel as though heavenly angels surged through my body and cleansed my soul. My pastor also seemed to had known all of the right things to say that re-enforced my beliefs of the LORD, which made me feel even closer to HIM.

There were tears of joy that over-came me when my other brother from Elgin, IL surprised me by being there to support me as I gave myself to the LORD.

What made it even more joyous was that my mother and the very close family whom I played "Amazing Grace" for at the gravesite were there.

There were two little young men at the age of ten along with me that also gave themselves to the LORD that day. Those two young men whom I am proud of and that thought so much of the LORD, at their age, really impressed me.

So, you whom are still tempted by the urge to continue to use that so-called "social drug" should take another look in the mirror and change that person that is reflected onto your face while you still have time. There is a better life ahead. You must only just want it bad enough to do something about it. Don't just only call for HIM when you are in trouble or in need. Call on HIM when you only need quiet talk. You will be amazed in what answers you may get.

If I had not changed my life from the use of that "social drug", I would not have been here today to get any blessings from the LORD. I was even blessed to play my flute for the LORD in church one week before my baptismal. All of these blessings that I am getting now are all new to me and I enjoy them to the utmost. It is all because I have given myself to the LORD and HE has given me a new beginning.

TRACT SIXTEEN

THE POINT OF NO RETURN

These next two articles I write are based on various ordeals that occurred during some of my most memorable experiences that still plague my brain cells. I have written so many articles that I failed to mention how I actually got started on that so-called "social drug". I didn't start by jumping right into the fire. It was a gradual progression that led to the usage of the "social drug". Actually, I never saw it coming because the drug took control so fast that it made the high speed roadrunner look like a slow snail going up a vertical hill.

First of all, I would like for you to take a moment to relax your mind and clear it of all other thoughts. Turn down the television or radio so that there will be silence in the room that you are now in. Take another look around to make sure that you will have at least five minutes of peace and quiet without being inter-rupted during this somewhat mental visual excursion.

And second, thank the LORD that you are able to read and comprehend these words that are in front of your face. You see, this "social drug" can also leave a mental defect within certain regions of your brain which will affect your ability to read, remember or your mobility functions.

Now, let's take a mental walk back into the past as I tell you about my first attempt to the use of the "social drug" in its powder form. This time, I will try to get you right in the scene with me so that you can make a judgment on: to do or not to do.

If I am correct, you will select the latter of the two choices. Picture this in your mind: you and I are going to pick up a package that is made from a corner of a plastic baggy, tied into a knot, with the white crystal powder about the size of a mini marshmallow. We just spent twenty dollars together on the package and now we are ready to go and snort it into our nose. Never realizing or thinking if it is good or bad stuff, yet we rush to a secluded place.

Once there, we pull out our paraphernalia; a mir-ror, a razor blade and a rolled dollar bill. We open the little baggy and empty the content on the mirror. There it sits on the mirror, sparkles of white powdered gran-ules looking like a crystallized ant hill. Next, we take the razor blade and cut down into the middle to split it into two almost equal parts. During all of this time that it was placed on the mirror, it was so quiet that one could hear a mouse's little paw nails tap along a wooden floor as it scurries to its little safe haven hole.

As we take the razor blade and make our second pass through the white powder we shave off a little to make long small narrow lines. Our next step is to make sure that our rolled dollar bill is tight and smooth on both ends on the insides. This will make it easier for the powder to be snorted up from the mirror to go directly into our nostrils.

Now, take the rolled dollar bill and insert it in one of your nostrils and take your finger and press close your other nostril, exhale, put the other end of the dollar down to the mirror where the long small line is and inhale quickly through your opened nostril with the dollar bill that is inserted....

SNOORRTTT !!! YOU NOW HAVE JUST RU-INED YOUR LIFE !!!!!!! You have just entered the "social drug" zone.

Your face is frozen from your top teeth up to your forehead, imagine what it has done to your brain. From this point on, there is no more control in your normal life. If you do it long enough, your nostrils will lose the hair, open the membranes and make them raw with sores inside that will bleed. This is how I got started on the powder and the blood from my nostrils made me change to the next level, which will be in the following article.

So, don't be another statistic of rehab or death. Len Bias was an up and coming professional basketball star which his first snort was his last. He died at the age of 22. Traces of cocaine were found in his body. One day before his death, the Boston Celtics had selected Len Bias second overall in the 1986 NBA draft. He celebrated by using cocaine (which was said to have been his first time), and he entered the point of no return.

It's your choice. I made mine.

TRACT SEVENTEEN

CHASIN A GHOST

n my last article you and I took a mental walk through one stage of addiction by way of snorting of the powder form of the "social drug". This time I would like for you to take another stage of addiction walk with me to the world of the glass pipe and the circulation white cloud; smoking of the "social drug". Keep in mind that this was a gradual transitional upgrade through years of its usage from the other form.

Again, clear your mind and find a quiet place to read without interruptions. We are about to embark into a new realm of the "social drug" activities that causes a people to lose respect for themselves.

The harmless looking white powder that seems to fascinate the human eyes like a dangerous spitting cobra. The cobra knows exactly where to spit to conquer its victim and the white powder has its way to conquer and turn a person into an addict.

"Do you have five on it?"- "I got five on it" - "I'll do it for five". These are the words that you will hear throughout the streets of a drug infested area. No respect for AIDS, NEEDLES, STDs or DANGER. They were all numb to the affect to these dangerous words.

Never-the-less, it was a continuous activity day into night, night into day. Women and men walking the streets trying to sell their bodies, items, drywall or even their kids to a dealer just to get another hit of that "social drug". I have seen it all from quick sex in a low lighted back alley inside abandon cars to orgies with up to ten participants in one room. IT"S NOT A GOOD SIGHT TO SEE!!!!

Imagine, if you will, a room full of hairless rats scurrying around trying to mate from one to the next as though it was their last day to eat or live. Now, walk with me through the horrors of smoking of the so called "social drug".

If you can remember that we had a total of twenty dollars between the both of us for a small plastic baggie of the white powder. This time, instead of snorting up it we will cook it up. First of all, we will need a test tube, baking soda, a little water, alcohol, cotton ball with a wire stem, copper scrubbing pad, a glass pipe and a lighter. (Paraphernalia)

With all of these items, it cost even more just to do the this form of "social drug" than it did to snort it.

Now that we've got all of the items that is needed, we are ready to continue our journey.

After combining the white powder and a little baking soda into the test tube with a small amount of water we begin to heat the bottom of the tube until it bubbles and clears. Add cold water, slowly shake until you see a formation of substance that will turn white. During this time, all eyes are hypnotized on the marvel of its wonders of creation. While in the tube, the substance will harden to a little white ball the size of a tiny candy jaw breaker.

From there we tilt the tube to let the little white ball roll to the top, releasing the water at the same time and then we will be able to place the white ball on a mirror (known as "the rock").

HOLD ON!, HOLD ON! We still are not ready to indulge yet. There is still more to do before we can actually get a chance to fire it up!

Now, we need to set up the pipe. ISN'T THIS A LOT TO DO BEFORE WE CAN ACTUALLY TRY IT? HUH? Are you having fun yet?

Ok! lets continue. We now need to take the copper scrubbing pad and burn it to clear the impurities out of the copper. Then we take some and stuff it into the pipe to make a screen.

NOW, WE ARE READY !!!! We will cut a piece of the rock and put it in the pipe on top of the screen. Take the cotton ball and twist it on the wire stem and dip it into the alcohol and light it. Bring it over to the pipe, inhale slowly while the flame is over the rock.

BEHOLD!!! The white cloud that circulates through the glass pipe which hypnotizes all that are in the room. Exhale, a fast rush within your body from head to toe. Your heart beats faster, your eyes opens wide, your brain senses the changes from normal to abnormal within seconds.

Your brain cells are now looking to be more satisfied with this foreign substance that just has invaded the body. Two minutes later it's all gone. The rush has subsided, your heart is back to normal with its beat and your eyes go back to a normal look - everything but your brain. Yes, your brain, it will never be the same. It wants more of that foreign stuff you just introduced it to. It wants to do that rush thing again.

The only thing about it is that, you can't get that same feeling again and now you are on your way to chasin' a ghost. Hit after hit, it will never be the same. You will end up doing it from dusk to dawn and you will never achieve the pinnacle.

Use your head! Don't go brain dead!

TRACT EIGHTEEN

A LESSON WELL LEARNED

n my last article I took you all through the horrid trip of "Chasin' a Ghost" and I tried to make you realize that the use of this "social drug" in that form is dangerous to your mind and body. Believe me, it is dangerous because I am a person who lived it.

Of all of the articles that I have written, they were all through my experiences with the "social drug" which has made me a stronger person along with the LORD'S help. If it had not been for HIM, I would not be here today.

January 30th, 1995 is a very special day for me in two ways. One way, it is my birthday and the other is, the day I decided to turn myself in to get help from that powerful "social drug".

I feel like a different man in all aspects of life. I have goals and most importantly, RESPECT for myself again. I want something out of life or whatever the LORD is willing to give me. As I stated before, I am HIS vessel and HE may use me as HE pleases. I don't have any trouble with it at all.

There is one thing that I failed to mention in "Chasin' A Ghost" and that it had transgressed to a new era that changed the ways of cooking your own rocks to ready made ones.

In this case the dealer would buy a large quantity of the powder form and would cook it all and cut it into different size pieces depending on the amount of money that a person would spend. From there he would put them in a plastic bag of different sizes. Doing it this way, would save time for the addict that was in a hurry to get his first hit. All an addict needed was a pipe, screens and a cigarette lighter. He would then be on his way much quicker.

I would get the ready rocks from the dealer when I wanted to get that fast rush as soon as I purchased them. I would walk out doors of the dealers place to an alley with my handy cigarette lighter, put on a piece of the rock on the pipe and light it. Off to the races I would go, "Chasin' a Ghost".

But, NO MORE will I never go through the drug changes again because I want to live with dignity. I like to be happy, and like being able to look back at the past and smile and laugh at the stupid things that I did while on the so-called "social drug". I couldn't laugh back then.

Ever since, I have been clean from the drug, I have no trouble with taking a drug test for any job that I pursue. I don't even mind talking about the things I used to do when I was an addict. I like for people to know that the "social drug" is not worth the hassles in life. Jail, tickets, no home, sleeping in abandon buildings and cars during the cold winters are terrible things to endure.

The fact of not being clean due to not wanting to because drug was more important. People looking down on you with whispers of bad talk towards you. It's no fun seeing and hearing people talk about you behind your back in how much of a dope addict that your are.

All of the things that I went through, it was a lesson well learned for me. It is something that I will never do again. Why should I keep falling into a deep hole when I know that I can go around it.

After being incarcerated many times due to the usage of this so-called "social drug" has made it much easier for me to stay clear from all whom that indulge simply because I care not to be in those situations again. I enjoy my freedom and the positive things that I do to improve my life.

The LORD has provided me with a chance to redeem myself from the horrid ways of life that plagued me in the past to pleasant and meaningful graceful blessings that I am grateful for. I will always thank the

LORD for the things that HE has let me do to change a homeless, shameless, and unforgivable creature like me.

I now stand erect with head held high, a proud strong man with gifts of golden experiences that I am willing to share with others. I no longer see that terrible man in the mirror that looked like death of skull and bones.

Thank you JESUS for all of the insights to become a better person to the eyes of my family and friends.

TRACT NINETEEN
FOREIGN MATTERS

When I think of all of the lessons that I have learned going through all of these ordeals, I realized that the LORD has blessed me with something worth more than gold.

HE has given me the opportunity to keep on living. HE also has bestowed me with the knowledge to stay off the so-called "social drug" and be HIS vessel to pass the word to the one's that are thinking of using this terrible drug. "DON'T USE IT !!!!".

No matter how a person would look at it, drinking, gambling, smoking or drug of choice, it is an addiction. It is indulging in a certain particular thing that causes the brain to want more which in turn damages the normal body functions.

Let it be known that; our bodies DO NOT belong to us. We are only using them on a temporary vessels because the LORD owns them. Why are we infecting our bodies with foreign matters that do not belong which aren't natural? As humans, we seem to not care that we are only using our bodies part-time. The LORD is the full-time owner of our sophisticated fine tune bodies that no human could ever think of creating. Once you are dead there is no need for a body.

As I look back on the things that I used to do by polluting my body with un-natural contaminates, it's a wonder that my brain, heart, limbs and inner organs still function as well as they do.

It is all because the LORD found fit for me to continue my life passing the word down to those whom indulge or thinking of trying this so-called "social drug". This brings in to mind of an ordeal that I went through when I kept polluting my body with foreign substances.

If you can recall, in one of my articles, when I was homeless and stayed out on the corner all night waiting for someone that I could trick out of their money for drugs but, got tricked myself.

Well, this was during that same evening when three so-called friends and myself found an old bottle of homemade wine in a basement that we were cleaning out for an elderly lady. Her husband had passed away and he tried his hand at making his own wine in the cellar. The wine had to have been sitting there for at least three or more years.

We decided to take the wine the lady was discarding and start drinking it. I had not eaten all that day and all I wanted was a hit from a rock, a smoke from a joint laced with cocaine and a drink from the aged wine. Little did I know that I was on the verge of an over-dose consuming all of that foreign matter that I was about to introduce into my body.

As I was standing on the corner with my so-called friends, I did all of the above and within five minutes my body started to change with different warning signs that I ignored.

Suddenly, my heart started to beat faster, my brain started to go in a way that my speech was slurred and my legs began to feel as though there was no blood in my lower extremities which it made it hard for me to stand on my feet.

PLOP! - I fell on the ground and my eyes started to wander out of control. I was short of breath and I could only think of it as being my last gasp for oxygen. ME, dying on the streets on the side of an old building, no identification or anything.

I tried to get up onto my feet by holding on to the building and tried to walk - two steps - PLOP!

I was down on the ground again. Again, I tried to get to my feet - three steps - PLOP! - to the ground I went with the fear of OD on my mind. I called for someone to help me but, they were too busy trying to get higher. I yelled, "CALL FOR AN AMBU-LANCE !" (in a slurred way)

They thought I was just playing around and they didn't realized that I was in need of help. It was more important to them to continue to getting high. I had to stagger to a fire station where they called an ambulance to take me to a hospital emergency room. After a multitude of testing and hours of waiting, the prognosis was, - too much drugs.

That day, I realized that ingesting foreign matters in my body via stomach, lungs or any sort through nasal will damage the normal actions of the delicate functions that a body goes through. Your body knows when there is something that it does not want there, it tries to reject it. If the substance it too over-powering for your body goes into shock and it shuts down.

That incident of being helpless, with no one to notice that I was on the verge of losing my life through the over-use of substances will forever be etched in my mind. The LORD gave me another chance to redeem myself and cleanse the impurities that had invaded my body due to ignorance and stupidity. Now, I have with the knowledge of understanding that my body does not belong to me. I am only using it for a few years and I need to keep it in good shape to continue to be mobile and do the things that HE wants me to.

All I need to do is let HIM be my guide.

TRACT TWENTY
THE LOST YEARS

Time - a four letter word that can span through centuries or even to a millisecond. It seems to be so small that it is insignificant to certain people that are really deep into the so-called "social drug".

I know this for a fact that time was not very important to me when I was involved with the "social drug". The only thing that was important to me at that time was getting another rock in a hurry and to get that one feeling that was so hard to come by; (the rush) which only lasted just a few minutes.

It was a rush and hurry state of mind when it came to the "social drug". Actually, to anyone that was into it, the faster you get that first hit before the next person the better one will feel the effect. You see, the cooler the pipe, the better the flow. The hotter the pipe, the less flow of the smoke and also the worst taste because it turns into a brown oily form.. This causes a person to start "chasin' a ghost".

Once you start, for example: nine a.m. in the morning and if your money holds out, you will be trying to reach that pinnacle all day into evening until nine or ten that same evening.

You will be so wired up that time seem to slip right on by without you noticing it. This brings into mind when I was deeply involved and it was on a pay day, Thursday, and I was on second shift. I would go in to my job early to get my check and then go cash it. Before I did anything else, like pay any bills I would go find and buy myself a few rocks. From there, it would be an all day affair into night or even into the next day. Time seems to stand still when you are indulging in the "social drug". It keeps you running around to and fro to the drug dealer, never realizing all of the time that has passed by.

You see, with all of the time that passed by day after day, hour after hour and minute after minute, when you finally take a look -Years have slipped by you without notice. You seem to forget there are other things that you can do such as: going to wash your clothes, take a bath or shower, visit your family, go to the grocery store for food or just plain saving your money in a bank. I know, because all of the ones I just mentioned, I have done.

I used to have plenty of money in the bank, but withdrew it all for the drugs. I even turned in my savings bonds down to my 401k savings. I never looked ahead and thought that my retirement would be affected by my stupidity.

All I wanted was another hit and to keep feeding the other addicts that were hanging around me for their portions. Just imagine, doing this same old stuff day after day for more than ten years and all of the money that was spent. I could have paid for the house that I once owned.

For some reason, the LORD let me fall on my face so that I could learn a lesson through experience. Experience is the true teacher of all. My Theory: "You can't teach it if you have not done it".

I was also too involved in the drug to even go to the store and buy groceries. If I did, I would only have enough to purchase three dollars worth of chicken wings and a small bag of rice. Both together was a big whopping amount of five dollars or less. Can you call this grocery? I wanted to make sure that I had "five on it" for the next rock. With me constantly spending my money on drugs, I could not even take the time out to visit my family. I didn't want them to see me in dirty clothes and not having taken a bath or shower.

I had just let time pass right on by me. Not a care in the world. I thought that I was content with this way of life, never utilizing time and money management. I could have been debt free at this time but, NO, I wanted to play ignorant to the fact that I was an addict. I just didn't want to face it because I thought that I had control over this so-called "social drug" .

Since I have been saved from the clutches of the drug, I continue to thank the LORD for what HE has done for me. It is amazing in what HE can do for you, if only you give HIM the chance. It is written that; "I can do all things through CHRIST, which strengthens me" I also realize that HE can not turn back the hands of time nor can I make up for the Lost Years.

I just love HIM for giving me, my life today. Thank you JESUS, my life is in YOUR hands.

TRACT TWENTY ONE
THE ROAD TO RECOVERY

Ever since my first article, "The Stages of a Dope Addict" was written, I realize that there were things that I could have added that would help someone else not use the "social drug". So, the articles that I will be writing now, I will try to go in depth starting from my very first one to the present. I only hope that what you all read will find a soft spot in your heart and go to your head so that you will stay away from this terrible drug.

When it comes to being a dope addict, it is hard to understand that one is lost with this dangerous chemical. The fact of being hooked is even harder to accept in the mind of a user.

You will think that you have it under control, but in reality the drug controls you. You will lose the respect that you once had from your family, friends and yourself. Standing up for yourself and by taking responsibility for your own actions will be a great start to a twelve step program for the road to recovery.

Picking your friends carefully and finding a Church to attend will give some insight on the right things to do. Asking the LORD for guidance and most of all, be willing to want to change your lifestyle will do a great deal in helping you. GOD is good. Trust in HIM. HE will take care of all your problems. Ever since I gave myself to the LORD, things has been going very well for me. I don't hang around the so-called friends that I used to be around and I stopped all activities of any drug use. I started liking myself again and I want better things out of life.

I had hit rock bottom. Living in abandon buildings and cars, eating once a day at Churches that served hot meals for the needy and standing on the corners all night are all behind me now thanks to the LORD and faith. I am not that shell of a man anymore. I now have a roof over my head, heat from the cold weather, two cars, a good job, started my own business, and among other things. Most importantly, I stay in constant contact with my family.

It feels really good to be around my family and good friends (real friends) again where I can laugh and be comfortable and not worry about where my next hit will come from or my next meal. I can also look in the mirror and see a real man standing tall with head held high. A proud man, and with a little more meat on my bones compared to the cross-bones and skull of death that I once saw.

Believe me, I have seen and done just about all there is when it comes to being a cocaine snorter to a smoker. The life a user leads only to bad things because it is illegal. There is no other way to go but downward when you are involved with this so-called "social drug".

For a woman, it is the worst thing because it makes them lose all respect for themselves. It makes them do sexually immoral things just for a small rock that's worth five dollars. These type of woman don't care if they get STD's. They will continue to pass it around within the circle of addicts without a second thought.

The most important thing is, trying to get high. If a man or a woman show that they have plenty of money or cocaine, the hooked woman will do all they can to be with that person until they spend it or smoke it all. This type of life makes a woman dope date anybody and be open to do anything sexually to keep them.

I have been there to see it all done in front of my face and I still find it hard to believe what I observed how that "social drug" changes an addicts personality. This drug had control over every fiber of their mind and body which lowered their ability to keep their self respect. I thank the LORD for letting me keep my sanity and not let me go down to those extremes.

To get away from all of that type of living, I decided to get help. I prayed to the LORD to guide me in the right direction to get me out of that environment. I turned myself into a hospital rehab center for three months and got all of the drugs out of my system.

From there, I learned all over again, how to love and have respect for myself. It even went as far as to having me to wash my dirty clothes and having good nutritional meals three times a day. Once released, I used the money that I had saved to get a motel with just one room that had a stove and refrigerator.

I would go back to work and do my eight hours and go straight back to the motel via bus transportation, staying away from the people that I used to hang around. I continued to work and save my money to be able to move into an apartment in a nice neighborhood that had two bed rooms, all new furniture throughout, new appliances which all are paid in full and a garage for my two cars. I am content and happy that the LORD gave me another chance in life. With HIS help, HE gave me the correct directions to the road to recovery.

TRACT TWENTY TWO
THE PATTERSONS

Sit down for just a moment and let me tell you a short truthful ordeal that I recently encountered. Are you sitting down? Find a nice quiet place so that this will absorb directly into your brain cells because it is short and to the point. First, you should know that, this article is dedicated to the Patterson Family of Milwaukee, WI. On, May 28, 2002, the Patterson family laid to rest her son. Just a little more than two years earlier, May 19, 2000 her husband passed away and was laid to rest. So much happened in the lives of the Patterson's in such a short time.

This is why I write this article because this could be someone close to you or in your family, and suddenly disappear forever within three to four days from last speaking to them. This is what happened to me after knowing this young man for about six and one half years, a former landlord, kind person that cared about the other tenants in the building. We would talk in the mornings when I come in from work and he would be going to work. He would always have that smile on his face.

This one particular morning, he was coming down the stairs and as usual, the same, "How are you this morning?" I asked, "What did you do to your leg? Trying to play basketball at your age? 'Limping and all".

But, there was a difference in his face this day. The smile was not as big. He said to me, "I think that I am having a stroke."

I replied, "No, you can' be not at your age". He responded, "I really do think so."

With a serious look on my face I said, "Then, I think you should go straight to the hospital and Right Now!"

After the ambulance arrived to take him to the hospital, I contacted his mother to let her know what just had happened. An hour later, I went to visit him and he seemed to be doing much better even though he only had limited use of his right leg and arm.

I talked to him and we had a joke or two for about a half hour. As I was about to leave, I turned to him and said, "Hurry and get out so that we all in the apartment can have you back on your feet and walking everyday to regain the strength that you lost.

He said to me, "It's just a minor set back."

By the time I got home almost an hour and a half, I got a call from his mother on my voice mail stating that he had a seizure along with a stroke. A couple of days later, he was gone.

All of my condolences went out to his mother because I can only imagine what it is like for a mother to bury her thirty-seven year old son; losing two loved ones within two years of the same month. With the ordeals she went through, I asked all I knew to say a prayer for her in her grief.

I was honored to photograph both funerals for Mrs. Patterson and asked GOD to continue to bless her throughout the years.

Now, look around you from left to right and see the people that are near and are dear to you. This could have been someone in your family. The LORD giveth and the LORD taketh away. Just thank the LORD each and everyday for letting you live on this earth to see another day as the sunrise or set.

Thank you JESUS for giving me life. LIFE is something one should not take for granted.

TRACT TWENTY THREE
BLINDED BY DENIAL

n my second article, I was trying to let you know that this so-called "social drug" will change any person no matter what creed, color, or ethnic background you come from. Once you get involve with this drug you will lose all respect for the way you live.

Through the years of my usage, I could not see where this drug was leading me. I was blinded by the need to use this so-called "social drug". I was in denial and I did not know it.

All I wanted was to get another hit of that powerful wonder drug that causes a rich man to go poor or make a very intelligent person to get trapped into the world of crack cocaine and go stupid. Judges, Senators, Movie Stars, and even Athletes all have fallen victim to this drug. Once it is tested, then you are hooked if you let it take control of your mind.

There is only one way to go when you start using this so-called "social drug" and that way is down. No ands, ifs, or buts about it, you will live a terrible life-style. If you like living on the edge, this is the best way to go out of this world backwards. Have faith in the LORD; HE is the only one that can save you from the realms of torture and despair.

If you don't want to live as another statistic on paper by being incarcerated, AIDS victim, or found dead in a garbage dumpster for you young girls trying to play grown up. The streets will kill you. You may think that all is well there in the streets, but home is the safest place to be.

If more than one person tells you that you have a problem, it is time to start thinking about getting some help. Even, if you hear it when people talk behind your back it is best to take time out and think of the circumstances that complements with this usage.

Face up to the fact that you have a drug problem, which is the first step on the road to recovery. You will be glad that you did. There is nothing like having freedom to go and come as you feel. Live your life to the fullest. Don't pollute the body that does not be-long to you. Just thank the LORD for letting you bor-row it for a while.

Ask the LORD if there is anything that can do for HIM because HE is always continuing to do things for all of us. I thank you JESUS for all that you do for this whole world and me.

It does not help if you try to cover a problem that will affect family or friends. Step up to the plate and be a strong person and regain you dignity. Don't be weak. Don't be blinded by denial.

TRACT TWENTY FOUR
UN-NAME THAT BULLET

The article that I will write about a little more in depth is my third one, which is called "A Bullet With No Name". If you all can recall, I was almost shot in the back of my head if I had not turned around in time.

To refresh your memories, I was sitting in my car with two "so-called friend dope dealers" and the one in the back seat pulled out his gun and pointed it in the back of my head. I had a strange feeling, something told me to turn around and when I did a gun was right there in my face where I could look straight down the barrel.

I was startled and quickly said, "Get that gun out of my face! " at the same time; I pushed the gun away with my wrist and POW!!! The gun went off. The bullet went through the front windshield between the other guy and myself. I was in a daze with the windows being up, I sustained powder burns on my wrist and forehead.

The flash powder burns was so hot on my forehead that I thought that I was shot with blood streaming down and was going to die. I saw my whole life go pass my eyes within seconds, from not seeing my family and kids anymore to the stainless steel table the coroners use for autopsy. I even saw them getting ready to cut me open (that's how fast your life can leave you). Almost dying for just another rock. What a horrid thought. They wanted to force me by gunpoint to drive them to get more rocks to sell.

Thanks to the LORD, HE saw a way for me to live another day. That was a warning right then and there. At that time I could not comprehend it. Thank you JESUS for protecting me through my days of hardships. YOU, let that bullet go right pass me and YOU, took my name off it.

Doing drugs is no game. It's all bad for you. You gamble with your life each day that passes by. Each day you get deeper and deeper to an unseen habit that may cause you to do the wrong things or may I say, "make the wrong choices". Don't be a victim of circumstances or a statistic with a bullet in your head and being found in a garbage dumpster or in a heavily wooded area. Be a survivor and don't let a bullet come to you with your name on it. Stand up and be strong. Don't use it!

You don't always die by the bullet. You can OD or even get strangled by an over-powering person of strength and/or possibly get hit on the head with a blunt instrument just for another hit of the rock.

Ask the LORD for help. HE controls "the bullets with no names".

Thank you JESUS again for being there for me when I was down and out, most of all, for un-naming that bullet that was supposes to have been for me.

TRACT TWENTY FIVE

THE SOUNDS OF FREEDOM

Darkness. The faint muttering sounds of voices that echo as they bounce off of the walls to the ever-listening ear, waiting impatiently for footsteps to come to the thick metal door.

The feeling of relief knowing that something is getting ready to happen when you hear the jingle of the keys as they about to unlock the massive lock tumblers within the thick metal door. As the door opens, a narrow beam of light shoots right in towards the floor where you see small dust particles floating as though they're dancing with grace in mid-air as the door opens completely. While the bars slide to the side, a rude awakening sets in motion.

"Get up! Get up! It's time to go". "Right now! Move it! Move it!" Coming from an overweight policeman that seems to have had too many doughnuts. As I grab my old black jacket and my shoestring less boots, I'm wondering where is he taking me, four a.m. in the morning. I had been there for three days already being charged for: MURDER ONE.

This experience is based on my fourth article. Keep in mind that there was a reason for the charges that were handed down to me. I thank the LORD for letting the truth come out which made me a free man today, which makes it possible to write these words.

MURDER ONE: two small words yet, a large piece to swallow when it is charged on your behalf. It all started when I was staying with a friend who was nice enough to let me stay in their home. The person knew that I was not clean from drugs because this person was doing them with me.

It was a very cold night with six to seven inches of snow. The house where I stayed was dark and the back door was opened. There were footprints in the snow coming and going from all directions. The door was normally left unlocked and closed by the person who owned the house whom let me stay there but, that night it was opened. This night was different, eerie and somewhat like a movie thriller episode.

It was early morning about 2:30am, and I wanted to get some sleep. As I slowly walked into the back door in the dark and up three steps into the kitchen there was no light from the small black and white television or the small plug-in night-light that goes in the electrical socket next to the bed. I stopped in my tracks halfway in the kitchen and I felt the hair on my nape rise, which made me think that I should be getting out of the house.

For some reason I felt as though that there was someone waiting in the dark ready to do damage to me. So, I quickly walked backwards to the door where the only light that I saw and left in a hurry. It was about a week or two later when I heard that the person was murdered and stuffed into the closet where my carrying bag and clothes were.

When the police found the person, blood had been all over my clothes and carrying bag which had all of my personal information inside. The police got my name and my mothers address and telephone number.

From the information the police got from my bag, they were on the search for me with a warrant for my arrest and I did not know it. Three to four weeks later, I was caught upstairs in another so-called friends home trying to get high and dragged off to jail for: MURDER ONE.

I still thank the LORD today for setting the records straight so that I can live a normal life outside the bars of a little 5ft x 7ft cell where you hear the echo sounds of footsteps and jingling keys that makes the tumblers unlock the door for me to be a free man again.

Thank you again JESUS for letting me see and hear the sounds of freedom.

TRACT TWENTY SIX
BRIGHT ORANGE
WAS ALMOST MY COLOR

The "Reason?" This was the question that was asked by me to myself, "Why am I being arrested?" " I didn't do anything!", was the statement that plagued my mind as I rode in the rear of the police patty wagon as I was transported to the downtown police precinct.

I was in plastic handcuffs that were tighten behind my back. The question kept entering my mind as though someone kept pushing the rewind/playback button in my brain.

As I rode with three other people that also had been arrested in the rear of the wagon, we were very talkative and asking questions to each other. Some questions were asked like: " What did you do?" "How did they catch you?" or "Did you do it?" Among us four, the questions went around, one stated, "Domestic violence" Another stated, "Strong arm robbery" The other one stated, "Theft". Everyone was smiling and made jokes until the question was ask to me. "What are you in here for?" When I stated what, an officer told me when I got near the patty wagon; I was being charged for, "MURDER ONE" (first degree homicide). All of a sudden, all jokes and smiles quickly disappeared and silence came in like a thick fog in London, England.

It had gotten so quiet that all we could hear was the rattles that were made by the wagon when it hit bumps in the street. They looked at me with as though I had swallowed a live rat whole. There were no more conversations in the wagon all the way downtown to the police precinct. As the wagon pulled into the underground entrance port I could hear sounds of policemen talking and laughing. The rear doors opens with the sound of keys jingling and then a loud voice shouts,

"Everybody get out! Hurry up! Move it, move it!" Since I was the last one to get in the rear of the patty wagon, I was the first one to get out.

As I was getting out and stepped on the rear ledge of the bumper an officer grabbed my arm and pulled me to the concrete pavement. I stumbled and still stayed on my feet. When I looked back at the wagon, the other officers were pulling the others out the same way as though they were trying to herd animals in a corral. They lined us up in one single file and pushed us forward toward the entrance doors of the jail. As we were walking in the doors, I looked around to my left and right and saw at least fifteen other men sitting with metal handcuffs connected to long benches. When I looked through the window behind the officers sitting at the desk that took our names and fingerprints along with a picture, I saw bright orange uniforms being worn by others that already had been through the induction desk.

There were different sections and areas which we were lead to. The first one was the metal detector, where they waved a black paddle shape over my entire body. As I moved to the next area, my picture was taken where I had to hold numbers underneath my chin. The next area was where they got my fingerprints. As I moved to the next area, they sent me to be measured for thong flipper shoes and bright orange overalls with COUNTY in big letters on the back.

After the measurements, they told me to go sit on the bench where they handcuffed me with the other men waiting for their new bright orange attire. The other guys that were sitting there asked what I did to be there and I told them, MURDER ONE, they tried to move over away from me as though I was a plague.

Within an hour after sitting there, an officer called my name to take me to a secluded small telephone booth looking cell from the rest of the people with a thick plastic window so that I can be watched from head to toe. About three hours later, they came and got me and took me to a psychiatrist to make sure that I wasn't suicidal. The psychiatrist told me that, "I had better find a good lawyer". And again, I stated, " I did not kill anyone" with a very serious expression on my face.

After a half an hour of interrogation, they sent me to a metal holding cell a long way from others without the bright orange suit that I was measured for and where I stayed for four days. On the forth day, the LORD saw fit for the police to find out the truth in who was the murderer and I was released on my own recognizance. I was very happy to get out of jail and be free. I noticed at that time that bright orange was almost my color.

TRACT TWENTY SEVEN
RAID IS NOT ONLY FOR BUGS

NEW JACK CITY!!! Three words. Three very strong words that can make a person change from living comfortable in a nice and clean cozy home to a poverty stricken roach infested, non-heated, non-clean environment.

A place where there are all sorts of strange people sitting, sleeping and do their drugs. This is a place where all types of drugs are used for smoking, snorting, shooting up or dope dating for any manner they would like just to get high. If one would have a chance to look around to see all of the misfits doing their thing in a place like this before you take that big step in drugs, it would change your mind on the spot.

Let me give you some insight on what you would see before you newcomers decide to make that big step into the world of drug usage.

Picture this. You walk into the door of an old ready to be condemned building. As you look around from left to right, you see all sorts of people doing their thing. One side would be shooting heroin into their veins and with belts tighten around their upper arms so that the veins would enlarge so that a needle could inject the drug into them. Within a minute or two, the person's eyes would slowly go into a mode of sleepiness as though it was a coma.

You look ahead there are at least five to six people sitting around a makeshift table of blocks or milk crates and a wooden board and a mirror with a white powdery substance shaped into lines with a razor blade where they would be snorting it up their noses.

And when you glance a little more around, you would see the same white powder being cooked in a test tube for smoking in a glass pipe. The only place that is somewhat closed off from the others with a sheet or blanket is for the use of dope dating just for the white rock.

If you could only imagine, fifteen to twenty people in one room all doing their thing like flies on a carcass, it would make you wonder if it is worth the trouble to get involved with the so-called "social drug" where there is no food nowhere in the place. You would see old needles, cans from beer on the floor along with cigarette butts and garbage in one corner as high as your knees.

With all of this in mind, there are people coming in and going out of the door every three to four minutes just to pick up more of what they like best. You never realize how much traffic there is until – BOOM! The door slams to the floor and police with bulletproof vests and black uniforms with rifles and pistols drawn, shouting "THIS IS A RAID! - HIT THE FLOOR! - AND DON'T MOVE AN INCH!"

This is known as a "smokehouse raid" where everyone gets a ticket or a free ride to the police station in a patty wagon with handcuffs as accessories.

For those that don't want to see what a jail cell looks like and being locked behind bars, stay away from drugs. Don't be a victim of circumstance in a raid that is meant for hard-core users.

Find something that will interest you in a positive manner. Think of goals that will benefit you and your family. There is no reason why a person can't go out and create a lifestyle that will make a better future for themselves.

I have been down to the lowest term in my life and when I asked the LORD to help me change and give me strength, HE was there for me all of the time and I did not know it. I prayed that I would get away from the drug scene and get a life that I could be proud of.

I don't want to see the roach infested, un-clean environment, almost condemned building with people running in and out all times of the night to early mornings. People sleeping on the floor in corners being walked over and fighting the roaches as they crawl near the garbage and back to their niches. The thing that really got me was how the roaches had gotten immune to being around the people and the drugs. The roaches seem to be addicted to the drugs because whenever someone put drugs on the table or start smoking, they would come out in herds to that spot.

The strange thing is, being in a raid in a condemned building is not fun and with this in mind you all must know that raid is not only for bugs. Some humans get it too.

TRACT TWENTY EIGHT

THE CRAZED GETAWAY DRIVER

Driving Miss Daisy. It sounds like a real slow drive through town sight seeing and enjoying the scenery. There's nothing to worry about. Just listening to the sounds of other cars going by as you drive fifteen miles per hour. With your eyes looking forward and every once in a while you gaze around without a care in the world. The sun beaming down through the windows of the car and your radio semi-blasted with the sounds of jazz and then suddenly, you hear police car sirens overpowering the music. You start to look around and think of trying to find a place to pull over to the right for safety.

All of a sudden, this big dark blue car drives by you at a high speed with three or four police cars in hot pursuit chasing it.

This scene is all too familiar to me because it was me that drove that big dark blue car trying to flee the capture of the police.

First of all, let me tell you how it all started. I was broke and hooked and I wanted another hit. My car was very low on gas and I didn't have two pennies to rub together so I was asked by two so-called friends to drive them on the south side of Milwaukee to where their job was located so that they could cash their checks. With me being so green and gullible to the tricks of an addict I agreed to drive them because I was promised gas and two rocks in return.

Little did I know that these two guys never had a job and they did not tell me. In fact, at that time I really didn't care because all I wanted was gas and another hit. As we were going on the south side they kept telling me that they had to pick up their checks and cash them at the store where they worked.

After we go to the store that sold food and liquor, they asked me just park in front and wait. They told me that they would only be in there for about three or four minutes, long enough to get the checks and cash them. The three or four minutes turned into about twelve to fifteen minutes.

I started to get impatient and was ready to go because I wanted that hit. So, I started the car and I pull it up to the doors to let them know that I was about to leave. And then suddenly one of them came out of the doors and got into the front seat. I asked, "Where's the other guy?" He stated, ("He will be out in a minute, he was right behind me.") With the car still running, that minute turned into another five. (Just to inform you that we were on the side of town where there were no Afro-Americans reside.)

All of a sudden, the other guy came out in a fast pace and jumped into the back seat and said, ("Go ahead drive off, hurry- go –go") in a frantic voice. As I looked back again, I saw two people come out of the doors after him. One was an employee and the other was a security guard. As they ran towards the car, one of them hit the trunk with his hand and the other took the number of my license plate. During this commotion, I asked with surprise, " What did you two do in there?"

I was stunned and with fear of being chased by the two employees in calling the police. Again, I asked, "What did you two do in there for them to chase you out of the doors?" The one guy in the back seat said, ("Keep on driving") and at the same time they started pulling big bottles of liquor out of their clothes and pants and putting them on the floor of my car. I shouted at them and said, "Get this stuff out of my car right now." So I pulled over and stopped the car and told them to get those bottles out right now. As they took them out and threw the bottles in some bushes I started to hear police sirens in the distance.

They got back in the car and I was going to drive back to the north side of town in a hurry. I was driving in somewhat of a high speed for about five to six blocks. We were surrounded by four to five police cars and wagons in a very short time. They came out from all directions, with tires squealing and doors slamming with their rifles and pistols drawn. They surrounded the car from all viewpoints aiming directly inside. They shouted with authority, "Get out of the car with your hands up!" We all were arrested and taken to jail and I was tagged as the "Get-a-way driver" and fined.

It was not a day of driving Miss Daisy. It was a day that I drove crazy. Lost through the needs of another hit. Believe me, for you whom would try walking the same route or may I say, driving the same route that I did, DON'T DO IT!

TRACT TWENTY NINE
THE ROAD TO NOWHERE

The thought of being without a home or a roof over your head is a scary and frightful feeling that I care not to endure again. Yes, I do mean again. I have been there and done that. Homeless and sleeping in abandon cars or condemned buildings during cold winters without heat. The only thing that kept me warm was an old sleeping bag that was given to me. I even had old clothes that I had laid out over the floor to make it softer to lye on.

For any of you that are willing to give up your hard earned money to a drug dealer, you should think twice before you step into the world of addiction. This type of addiction will make you lose your self-respect, respect from your family and friends and more importantly, where you reside. Without a home or an apartment you cannot receive mail or put an address down on an application for a potential job.

The main reason why I say this is because; I have gone through this ordeal already in my lifetime. I had to ask someone that lived in a home if I could use their address and telephone number so that I could receive information on general assistance aide. I would even go to different churches to try and get food from the pantry. Even there, I needed an address. Some churches would feel sorry for me and let me have a small bag of food to last for a couple of days without an address and they would tell me, "next time you will need to have an address" before I could get anything else from them.

There was even a time that I wanted to give blood for money. I couldn't do that because I had no valid identification due to not having a valid address. So, they turned me down and therefore I could not give blood for money. If I had gotten the money, I would have used it for another hit. That was the main reason why I wanted to give blood.

I am so glad that the LORD kept his hand on me through my times of homelessness because, where I stayed was really dangerous. I would pull the board off of an entrance during the dark of night never knowing who or what would be in there. Even when I would try to get some sleep, I would never know if someone would come into the building that has echoes of hollow sounds that bounces off of the walls.

When the morning came, I would go out of another side of the building so that I would not be seen and start a new day of looking for aluminum cans to collect so that I could turn them in for money for another hit. I would also take time to go to the churches for the free hot meal program and then continue on my journey for more cans.

I finally can to the conclude that I chose to live this way because I was just only a fresh new drug addict and could not control my actions being hooked on cocaine and the marvels of watching the smoke swirl through a glass pipe which only gives a two minute high, if that long.

If it had not been for the LORD and my willing to change my ways, I would not be here today trying to stop another person from going through the same things that I did. So, for those of you are thinking of using the rock; "Think Long and Think Hard", because you will be taking the wrong road to nowhere. Being homeless is a dangerous road to take. It leads to nowhere.

TRACT THIRTY

FROM PAST TO PRESENT

S ince January of 1995 I have had big changes in my life. From a shell of a man and back to having respect for myself. I went from being a hard working family man in 1976 to a homeless skeletal of a man in 1982 to January 1995. I came back as a skilled welder with a diploma, a photography business, a musician and finally finding my way to being a man of God. I am married to a wonderful woman of God, Pamela (aka: P. Utley Bradford - author).

Even through those years, I still had trials and tribulations to confront to get to where I am today. It took faith and determination to keep my mind busy doing good things. I would like for you, readers to take this last journey with me sit back and relax for awhile as you read this last article and mentally experience the trials and tribulations into my life as I struggled to change my attitude to a better person that I am today.

During the years before 1995, it was hard to get drugs out of my mind. I kept thinking that I had control of the drug at that time. I thought that I could go get a rock and take it back to my motel room, that I had rented by the month and get my high on without any repercussions.

The only thing, I was only fooling myself. I already had ended up losing my first and second wife over sex, drinking and drugs. In my mind I knew I would be only heading back to homelessness if I would have taken that first hit again after being out of treatment center only months earlier.

The Lord must have had a plan for me back then and I didn't know it. After the long talks I had with myself and with God, I decided to follow the Lords path so that I could come out of the foolish life that I was leading.

I almost got fired from my welding job where I had been employed since 1976. My livelihood was in jeopardy. I started making adjustments in my thinking, so that I would not lose all of my retirement benefits which would make it hard for me to keep food in my stomach, roof over my head and transportation to places that I needed to go to .

As a couple of months slowly passed by, I was able to clear my head and realize that I could not hang around the same people that I was getting high with. Getting high wasn't fun anymore. The people I was getting high with would start hanging around each exit gate on my payday expecting for me to buy cocaine for them like I use to. They kept me broke by spending on myself and them instead of paying my bills.

The truth was, that I was weak minded and wanted to get high, so I found different places to hide to get peace alone to enjoy the high that I worked so hard for. Yes, the fun was gone. I asked the Lord to help me to get rid of that skeleton in the mirror and be the man I was before I got into the "social drug". After losing the desire to entertain the "social drug", I decided to set goals for myself.

After the company which I was employed since 1976, moved to Mexico, the employer paid for employees that were affected, by paying tuition for college for associate degree programs.

I decided to take them on the offer and go back to college. I had not been in college since 1969, straight out of high school. So, I put my best foot forward and prayed to God to help me do the right thing. I got my Associate Degree by getting a welding diploma and I was a honor student graduate.

And I didn't stop there. I continued to get more involved in my hobbies to improve my skills with my photography business since 1997 and still going today. Also during that time, I spent many hours practicing on my flute and drums, which I had started when I was fourteen and had a band.

I took my flute just about everywhere I went, even to the army in 1970. Today, I play my flute for the Lord at different churches am looking forward to producing a CD.

And with a special thanks to NEO and with the help of his publishing company "TRUBUPRESS", this book is in your hands to read and learn from my mistakes. Find your gift and take time to listen to the words from God's testimony in my life.

I'd like to give honor to God, who is the head of my life. To my wife, P. Utley Bradford, that has been with me since 2007 in marriage and known each other since childhood along with her children. To my oldest brother, Percy, a retired ironworker, who showed me different views in life and got me to Milwaukee, WI from a small hometown of Champaign-Urbana, IL.

To my sister, Lillie, a retired secretary from a health clinic in C-U, IL, who stuck by my side and listened to my deepest wounds and trials in my life through my drug addiction. To my other brother, C.R., who gave me the ideas of higher education where we attended college, Eastern Illinois University, Charleston, IL. He was the dean of Alpha Phi Alpha fraternity which I am also a member and now he is a retired Principle of a high school from Elgin, IL.

To all of my kids, even the ones that don't accept me as their father because of my absenteeism during my drug addiction and one oldest son that was given up for adoption when I was at a young age of 15 years old, "YOU ALL WERE LOVED" within my heart. Thanks to my uncles and aunts that are still here today. For my mother and father that are with the Lord now since 2007 and 1966 respectively, thank you for having me. I wouldn't be here today if it weren't for you two.

And thanks to all who took part in my life to guide me forward, my Bishop's and Pastor's from C-U, IL to Milwaukee, Cynthia Utley, who got me started in writing articles for her newsletter from Decatur, IL church. Thanks to cousins, friends, neighbors and all I fail to mention, God knows my heart. And last but not least, the U.S. mail lady carrier, Tina who was a witness in one of my articles, "A Bullet with No Name".

God has taken me through different stages of life to make me a better man. He has let me survive through two different cancers both with surgeries and now I am cancer free.

Thank you, Jesus. I am elated to be alive today.